Artists in Their World

Salvador Dalí

Robert Anderson

FRANKLIN WATTS
LONDON • SYDNEY

This edition 2005

First published in 2002 by
Franklin Watts, 338 Euston Road
London NW1 3BH

Franklin Watts Australia
Hachette Children's Books
Level 17/207 Kent St
Sydney NSW 2000

© Franklin Watts 2002

Series Editor: Adrian Cole
Series Designer: Mo Choy
Art Director: Jonathan Hair
Picture Researcher: Diana Morris

A CIP catalogue record for this book
is available from the British Library.

ISBN 0 7496 6629 3

Dewey Classification Number 759.6

Printed in China

Acknowledgements

The Advertising Archives: 40. AKG London: 12t. Archive Photos/Hulton Archive : 20tl. Archivio
Iconografico, S.A: Corbis 11 © Salvador Dali, Gala-Salvador Dali Foundation, DACS, London 2002.
Bettmann/Corbis: fr cover bc,19b, 32b. Central Press/Hulton Archive: 25t. Fox Photos/Hulton Archive:
32tl. Daniel Frasnay/AKG London: 20cr, 42. Fundació Gala-Salvador Dalí : 6, 7b, 9t © Salvador Dali, Gala-
Salvador Dali Foundation, DACS, London 2002, 13 © Salvador Dali, Gala-Salvador Dali Foundation,
DACS, London 2002, 33 © Salvador Dali, Gala-Salvador Dali Foundation, DACS, London 2002, 39 ©
Salvador Dali, Gala-Salvador Dali Foundation, DACS, London 2002. © Fundacion Federico Garcia Lorca:
12b, 14t. Galerie Daniel Malingue, Paris: Bridgeman 18t © ADAGP,Paris and DACS, London 2002. Robert
Harding PL: 7t, 8. Charles Hewitt/Picture Post/Hulton Archive: 22bl. Hulton Archive: fr cover br,18b, 24b,
30tl, 34, 36b. Courtesy of Kobal Collection: 16tl, 17, 35b. Kunsthalle, Hamburg: Bridgeman 10 © DACS
2002. Louvre, Paris: Bridgeman 14b, Giraudon/Bridgeman 30c. Courtesy Lee Miller Archives: 28t. Museum
of Modern Art, New York: Artothek fr cover c & 21 © Salvador Dali, Gala-Salvador Dali Foundation,
DACS, London 2002, 23 © Salvador Dali, Gala-Salvador Dali Foundation, DACS, London 2002. Musée
National d'Art Moderne, Paris: Lauros-Giraudon/Bridgeman 35t © ARS, NY and DACS, London, 2002.
Musée d'Orsay, Paris: Bridgeman 22t. Philadelphia Museum of Art: Corbis 28b. Prado, Madrid:
Giraudon/Bridgeman 26b. Private Collection: Index/Bridgeman 15 © Salvador Dali, Gala-Salvador Dali
Foundation, DACS, London 2002 : Lauros-Giraudon/Bridgeman 24t © ADAGP, Paris and DACS, London
2002. Rex Features: 41t. Ewa Rudling/Sipa Press/Rex Features: 41b. St Mungo Museum of Religious Art,
Glasgow: Artothek 37 © Glasgow Museums: The St Mungo Museum of Religious Life & Art. Sipa
Press/Rex Features: 36b, 38. Tate Picture Library: 26t detail © Salvador Dali, Gala-Salvador Dali
Foundation, DACS, London 2002, 27 © Salvador Dali, Gala-Salvador Dali Foundation, DACS, London
2002, 29 © Salvador Dali, Gala-Salvador Dali Foundation, DACS, London 2002, 31 © Salvador Dali,
Gala-Salvador Dali Foundation, DACS, London 2002. Topical Press Agency/Hulton Archive: 16tr.

Whilst every attempt has been made to clear copyright
should there be any inadvertent omission please apply
in the first instance to the publisher regarding rectification.

**THE GODOLPHIN AND LATYMER SCHOOL
IFFLEY ROAD, HAMMERSMITH
LONDON W6 OPG**

TELEPHONE: 020-8741 1936
FACSIMILE: 020-8746 3352

This book is due for return on or before the date last
stamped below unless an extension of time is granted

Contents

Who was Salvador Dalí?   6

An artist from Catalonia   8

Studying in Madrid   10

Close friends   12

Painting from life   14

Making a Surrealist film   16

Surrealism   18

To confuse and disturb   20

Love and marriage   22

The Spanish Civil War   24

The horror of war   26

Star of the show   28

Painting the unconscious mind   30

The power of Hitler   32

Dalí in the United States   34

The man with the moustache   36

The final performance   38

Dalí's legacy   40

Two Catalan Surrealists   42

Timeline   42

Glossary   44

Museums and galleries   45

Index   46

Who was Salvador Dalí?

Salvador Dalí was born Salvador Felipe Jacinto Dalí Domènech on 11 May 1904 in Figueres, a town situated in a region of northeast Spain called Catalonia.

Dalí's father, also called Salvador, was an important and respected person in Figueres. He had many friends in the town, some of whom were writers or painters. Dalí's mother, Felipa, was a pious Roman Catholic. She was loving and very warm-hearted. Dalí later described her as the 'honey of the family'.

'At the age of six I wanted to be a cook. At seven I wanted to be Napoleon. And my ambition has been growing steadily ever since.'

Salvador Dalí

▲ Salvador Dalí, aged 5, in a park in Barcelona. As a boy, Dalí was pampered and spoiled. His elder brother died while still a baby, less than a year before Dalí's birth, so his parents were particularly protective of their second son.

DAY-DREAMER

The young Salvador and his younger sister, Ana María, spent most of their childhood in and around the comfortable family apartment in the bustling centre of town. Between the ages of 6 and 12, Salvador went to a Roman Catholic primary school run by French priests. He was very intelligent, though he found it difficult to concentrate on his work during lessons. He often found himself day-dreaming in the classroom. Sometimes he doodled over his school books. At other times, he simply stared at the stains of damp on the classroom ceiling made by the leaky roof, and imagined they were all sorts of wonderful things.

NATURAL INSPIRATION

At weekends and during the long, hot summer holidays, the Dalí family went to the seaside village of Cadaqués. There they had a house surrounded by beautiful gardens, fields and orange groves. Salvador and Ana Mariá spent their days exploring the rock pools and beaches, or watching their father's friends painting the breathtaking views across the Mediterranean Sea. The Dalís' house was always full of aunts, uncles and cousins, as well as many other guests. Yet despite this apparently idyllic life, Dalí remembered his childhood as sometimes troubled and unhappy.

▲ The picturesque fishing village of Cadaqués remained Dalí's favourite place throughout his life. Its beaches and cliffs feature in many of his paintings.

▲ The Dalí family at Cadaqués in about 1910. Left to right are Dalí's aunt Mariá Teresa, his mother and father, Salvador himself, his aunt Catalina, his sister, Ana Mariá, and his grandmother Ana.

MEMORIES AND MYTHS

In 1942, Dalí published his life story, or autobiography, which he called *The Secret Life of Salvador Dalí*. In it, Dalí made up many stories about his childhood. For instance, he wrote that his older brother had died aged seven and that his parents always loved his brother more than him. In fact, his brother died when still a baby. Dalí saw nothing wrong in making up such stories. He claimed that they told an 'emotional' truth that went far deeper than simple facts. All the same, Dalí certainly had a difficult relationship with his father.

An artist from Catalonia

▲ One of the most astonishing sights the young Dalí saw in Barcelona was the church of the Sagrada Familia designed by Antonio Gaudí. The church's 'melting' shapes helped inspire Dalí's Surrealist masterpieces.

Dalí's father often took him to Barcelona, the Catalan capital. At the time, the city was flourishing, and there were exciting new buildings and parks to see, many designed by the famous architect Antonio Gaudí (1852-1926). His most extraordinary building was the Sagrada Familia (Holy Family), a church so vast and extravagant that it is still not finished today.

Barcelona had many lively cafés. One of the most popular was els Quatre Gats. There painters and writers gathered to discuss the latest ideas from Paris. At the time, Paris was at the forefront of new developments in art and many Spanish artists, including Pablo Picasso (1881-1971), lived and worked there.

VIOLENCE AND TRAGEDY

In spite of its prosperity, Barcelona was sometimes rocked by unrest and violence. The city's many factory workers were usually poorly paid and badly treated. Some supported the socialist and communist ideas of the German thinker Karl Marx (1818-83); others supported anarchism – the belief that people should be able to live their lives free of the laws of the government and the church.

TIMELINE ▶

11 May 1904	1907	1908	1909	1914	1914-1918	1917
Salvador Dalí Domènech is born in Figueres, Catalonia, Spain.	The Spanish artist Pablo Picasso paints his first Cubist pictures in Paris.	Dalí's sister, Ana Mariá, is born.	The 'Tragic Week': workers strike in Barcelona.	Gaudí's Güell Park opens in Barcelona.	World War I; Spain does not take part.	Dalí holds an exhibition of his paintings in the family apartment.

▲ *Portrait of My Father*, 1920. Dalí painted this portrait aged 16. The shimmering colours and lively brushstrokes clearly show the influence of a group of French artists known as the Impressionists.

In 1909, many Barcelona workers rose up against the government and burned down churches and schools. The army put down the uprising, and 116 people died. Catalans still remember this terrible event as the 'Tragic Week'.

YOUTHFUL PROMISE

Anarchist and socialist ideas were popular among Dalí's classmates, but he chose to concentrate on what he loved best – drawing and painting. He started to draw and paint as a very young boy. His parents encouraged him and even gave him his own studio. At the age of 13, Dalí won a prize for his drawing, and his proud father threw a party to celebrate. Dalí's early paintings included seaside views of sailing boats, whitewashed houses and green olive groves. He also made portraits of his father, whom he often showed wearing a smart suit and a heavy gold watch and chain. Even as a teenager, Dalí experimented with the bold new styles from Paris.

CATALONIA

Until the 18th century, Catalonia was an independent country, separate from Spain. To this day, Catalonia's people – the Catalans – remain very proud of their local traditions and customs, including their own language, Catalan. Dalí's father was a strong supporter of Catalan culture. Catalan was spoken in the family home, although Dalí was taught to speak Spanish and French as well. Throughout his life Dalí was proud of his homeland and he often wore a *barretina* (see page 36), a traditional Catalan soft hat.

Catalonia's landscape comprises a great rugged plain and a long coastline of rocky beaches, washed by the warm Mediterranean Sea. Catalonia's capital, the port of Barcelona, is on the coast. Dalí was born in the town of Figueres, which lies in the far north of Catalonia, about 97 kilometres northeast of Barcelona. This small, prosperous town nestles at the foot of the Pyrenees Mountains, not very far from Spain's border with France.

▲ Catalonia lies in the northeast corner of Spain. The surrounding mountains and sea long helped to keep the region apart from the rest of the country and gave it a strong separate identity.

Studying in Madrid

In 1922, Dalí, now 17, went to the Spanish capital, Madrid, to study at the San Fernando Academy of Fine Art. Dalí quickly became unhappy with the teaching given by the academy's professors. He preferred to wander round Madrid's huge art museum, the Prado. There he admired the works of the great Spanish painters, including Diego Velázquez (1599-1660) and Francisco de Goya (1746-1828). He also kept close contact with the latest developments in modern art.

◀ *Melancholy: The Street*, Giorgio de Chirico, 1924. In this painting, de Chirico uses a traditional, realistic style to create a disturbing image of a small girl running down a deeply shadowed street.

AN ECCENTRIC STUDENT

In Madrid, Dalí lived in a university residence. There he met a group of radical young writers and painters, including the poet Federico García Lorca (1898-1936) and Luis Buñuel (1900-83). The students led a riotous life in Madrid's cafés and night clubs. Dalí became known as an eccentric. One of his favourite tricks was to let a banknote dissolve in a glass of whisky before he drank it!

NEW KINDS OF ART

During and after World War I (1914-18), many European painters grew tired of the endless experiments of the previous decades and began to paint in much more traditional ways. Artists such as the Italian Giorgio de Chirico (1888-1978) rejected the bold colours used by the Expressionists and the shattered shapes of the Cubists. Instead, they painted in a straightforward fashion, using sober colours and conventional techniques such as perspective. Often, however, they put these old styles of painting to new uses, creating startling or even disturbing images. Dalí found this approach very attractive.

TIMELINE ▶

1917	February 1921	October 1921	1922	October 1922	1923
Revolution in Russia brings about the world's first communist government.	Dalí's mother dies.	Dalí goes to Madrid to study at the San Fernando Academy of Fine Arts.	The Surrealist group forms in Paris, led by André Breton.	Benito Mussolini becomes Fascist dictator of Italy.	Sigmund Freud's *The Interpretation of Dreams* is published in Spanish.

Portrait of Luis Buñuel, 1924

oil on canvas 68.5 x 58.5 cm Museo Nacional Central de Arte Reina Sofía, Madrid

Luis Buñuel was one of Dalí's closest friends at his student residence in Madrid and later became a famous Surrealist film-maker. In his portrait, Dalí shows his friend standing in a strange wintery landscape and uses only a few gloomy colours and shades – brown, grey, black and white.

Close friends

▲ Picasso in his studio in 1929.

DALÍ AND PICASSO

For Dalí, Pablo Picasso was the greatest living painter. At the beginning of the 20th century, Picasso helped pioneer a revolutionary new art known as Cubism. A Cubist painting shows several views of a subject – such as a person or still life – at once. During the 1920s, Dalí produced his own Cubist pictures, including *Pierrot Playing the Guitar*.

Picasso saw and praised Dalí's exhibition at the Dalmau. And, in 1926, Dalí visited Paris for the first time. Almost at once, he went to visit Picasso at his studio. On meeting him, Dalí declared: 'I have visited you before going to the Louvre.' The Louvre is one of the world's greatest art museums!

In 1923, a Spanish general named Miguel Primo de Rivera set up a dictatorship in Spain. Dalí's father opposed the regime, and the government took revenge by sending his son to prison for 35 days. The young Dalí did not seem to mind very much and spent his time drawing and drinking wine.

POETRY AND PAINTING

Dalí's closest friend during the 1920s was the poet Federico García Lorca. Lorca came from the hot, sunny region of Andalucía, in the far south of Spain. His poetry is full of passion and dreamlike images. The two friends admired each other's work deeply and each felt that their art evolved as a result of their friendship. They grew so close that Dalí thought of himself and Lorca as almost a single person, as he showed in *Pierrot Playing the Guitar*.

◀ Dalí (left) and Lorca (right) in Cadaqués. After his first visit there, Lorca wrote a poem in praise of Dalí.

'May stars like falconless fists shine on you, while your painting and your life break into flower.'

Federico García Lorca, from his Ode to Salvador Dalí

In 1925, Barcelona's most important art gallery, Dalmau, gave Dalí his first exhibition. The critics wrote favourably about the young new artist, and Dalí sold many paintings. He sent Lorca his bad reviews only, saying: 'the others aren't of interest because they are so enthusiatic.'

TIMELINE ▶

September 1923	October 1923	May 1924	October 1924	March 1925	November 1925	April 1926
Miguel Primo de Rivera sets up a dictatorship in Spain.	The San Fernando Academy suspends Dalí.	Dalí serves a one-month prison sentence.	Breton launches the first *Surrealist Manifesto* in Paris.	Lorca goes with Dalí to Cadaqués. Close friendship develops.	The Dalmau Gallery holds Dalí's first solo exhibition.	Dalí makes his first trip to Paris and visits Picasso and Joan Miró.

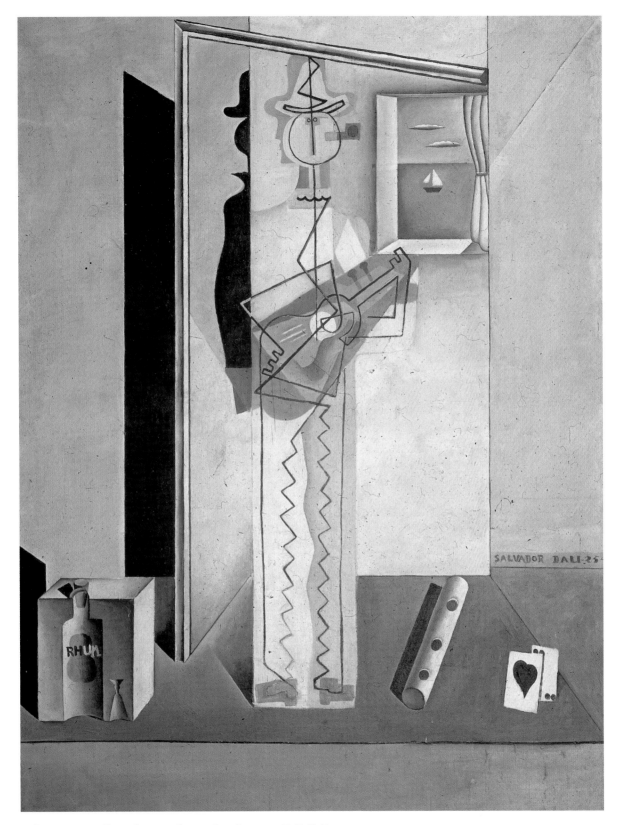

Pierrot Playing the Guitar, 1925

oil on canvas 198 x 149 cm Museo Nacional Central de Arte Reina Sofía, Madrid

Pierrot was a clownlike character from French pantomimes and features in several of Picasso's paintings. In this picture of Pierrot, Dalí mixed up his own features with those of his friend Lorca. On the floor are a bottle of rum, a flute and some playing cards. The ace of hearts suggests the tender friendship that united the two men.

Painting from life

Dalí did not concentrate purely on one style of art in his early years. In developing his art, he imitated – and experimented with – many different styles and was open to influences both from avant-garde painters and the Old Masters of the past.

PAST MASTERS

Throughout his life, Dalí admired the great artists of the past. One of his favourite pictures was *The Lacemaker* by the Dutch artist Jan Vermeer (1632-75). This tiny painting shows a girl working intently on a delicate piece of lace. Lacemaking requires skill and patience and was traditionally done by women at home. Vermeer's beautiful painting inspired Dalí to paint his own sister at work on a piece of lace.

A MODEL SISTER

Dalí spent his holidays from the Madrid academy at home at Figueres or at the seaside at Cadaqués. His paintings of this time often showed his sister – looking out across Figueres harbour or quietly working, for example. He also painted still lifes – pictures of everyday objects, such as fruit and bread, knives and bottles.

▲ Dalí with Ana Mariá in Cadaqués, 1925.

EXPELLED

In October 1926, Dalí was expelled from the San Fernando Academy shortly before graduating. He refused to do a part of his final examinations. His excuse was that he knew more than his examiner. Perhaps he was right – he already had a growing reputation and his work had attracted the attention of not only Picasso but the Catalan artist Joan Miró (1893-1983). However, Dalí's extraordinary self-confidence and even boastfulness were an important part of his personality.

◀ *The Lacemaker*, Jan Vermeer, 1669-70.
Vermeer's painting is less than 25 cm high. Its intricate detail matches the painstaking work of the servant girl.

TIMELINE ▶

October 1926	January 1927	February 1927	June 1927	September 1927
Dalí is expelled from the San Fernando Academy.	Dalí has his second one-man show. Includes *Woman Sewing at a Window in Figueres*.	Dalí begins 9 months' military service based in Figueres.	Lorca's play *Mariana Pineda* opens in Barcelona, Dalí designs set and costumes.	The Catalan Surrealist artist Joan Miró visits Dalí and later writes to encourage him to move to Paris.

Woman at the Window Sewing in Figueres, 1926

oil on canvas 24 x 25 cm Private Collection

Ana Mariá sits on a balcony overlooking Figueres's main square. Beyond are the blue Pyrenees Mountains. The budding trees tell us it is the beginning of spring. Like Vermeer, Dalí shows us just what it feels like to be deeply absorbed in a task – whether it is lacemaking or painting.

'Those who do not want to imitate anything produce nothing.'

Salvador Dalí

Making a Surrealist film

In the late 1920s, Dalí became increasingly attracted to the art of the Surrealists, and experimented with their strange, dreamlike images. The Catalan Surrealist Joan Miró encouraged Dalí to go to Paris. Once there, Miró told him, he would find success.

▲ A poster for *Battleship Potemkin*, a film directed by Sergei Eisenstein.

MONTAGE

In their film, Dalí and Buñuel used a new technique called montage to startle the audience. In film-making, montage means a rapid succession of different images. The pioneer of montage was Russian film-maker Sergei Eisenstein (1898–1948). Earlier film-makers had simply let the camera run, so that watching a film was like watching a play at the theatre. In the 1920s, Eisenstein developed a way of editing together different shots to make his films more gripping, quickly cutting from one viewpoint to another.

▲ During the 1920s and 30s, Paris was the artistic capital of the world.

INSPIRED BY DREAMS

In early 1929, he began working on a Surrealist film with his old college friend Luis Buñuel. The film was inspired by their dreams. Buñuel's dream was of a cloud slicing the moon in half, while Dalí's was of a hand swarming with ants. In April, Dalí went to Paris to shoot the movie with Buñuel. The film was called *Un chien andalou* (*An Andalusian Dog*).

Un chien andalou was quite unlike any other film made before and attracted a great deal of attention – it ran for 8 months at a cinema in Paris! It is only 17 minutes long, and there is hardly any plot. Instead, the film is made up of a series of dreamlike images – including a hand crawling with ants and a dead donkey lying over a grand piano.

TIMELINE ▶

March 1928	April 1929	Summer 1929	October 1929	November 1929
Dalí publishes the *Yellow Manifesto* denouncing Catalan art.	Dalí goes to Paris to make the film *Un chien andalou* with Luis Buñuel.	Dalí begins affair with Gala Éluard, wife of Surrealist poet Paul Éluard (1895-1952). Dalí's father bans him from the family home.	*Un chien andalou* opens to the public in Paris. The Wall Street Crash: economic depression hits the United States and Europe.	Dalí has his first exhibition in Paris.

Still from *Un chien andalou*, 1929 – hand crawling with ants

This is just one of many strange and unnerving images in Dalí and Buñuel's film. Another scene includes shots of a cork, a melon, two Roman Catholic priests, and two grand pianos on each of which is a dead donkey. Dalí included ants in many of his paintings. For him they were a symbol of death and decay. As a child, he had rescued a bat but later found it dead and swarming with ants.

'Why ... did a black hole appear in the middle of my palm, filled with a swarming anthill that I try to scoop out with a spoon?'

Salvador Dalí

Surrealism

Un chien andalou firmly established Dalí at the centre of the Surrealist movement. The Surrealists liked the film because it used many of their ideas.

INTERPRETING DREAMS

The Surrealists explored the world of dreams. They were not the first artists to do this, but they were the first to take much of their inspiration from the Austrian thinker Sigmund Freud (1856-1939). In his book *The Interpretation of Dreams* (1900), Freud showed how a psychiatrist could help people solve their problems by analysing, or interpreting, their dreams. Freud believed dreams could reveal the unconscious mind.

▲ *Dialogue of Insects*, Joan Miró, 1924-25. André Breton called Miró 'the most surrealist of all'. This painting is typical of Miró's work in the 1920s, full of joyous colours and childlike imagination.

BETTER THAN REAL

'Surreal' was a made-up word, meaning 'more than real' or 'better than real'. The leader of the group was the French poet André Breton (1896-1966). In 1924, Breton organised the publication of the first *Surrealist Manifesto*, outlining the group's ideas. The first exhibition of Surrealist paintings took place in Paris in 1925, and included works by the German Max Ernst (1891-1976) and Joan Miró. Soon many other artists in Europe and the United States took up the Surrealists' ideas. Dalí belonged to this second, younger generation. The older Surrealists, including Breton, quickly recognised Dalí's importance.

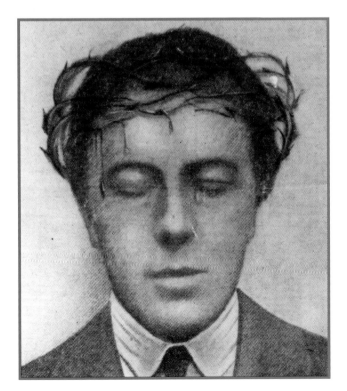

◀ André Breton as he was pictured in the first Surrealist Manifesto in 1924.

UNCOMFORTABLE ART

The Surrealists disliked much of the art of their time because they felt it was too cosy and comfortable. They particularly despised the work of the French painter Henri Matisse (1869-1954). Matisse once declared that a good painting should be just as soothing as 'a good armchair'. By contrast, the Surrealists wanted to shock and unsettle the people who looked at their pictures, forcing them to think rather than just look.

One way the Surrealists did this was to put objects together in unusual combinations – for example placing a donkey on a piano, as Dalí and Buñuel did in *Un chien andalou*. Sometimes the Surrealists did this using collage, combining photographs and words cut out from newspapers and magazines. Another Surrealist technique was frottage. This involved making rubbings of a floorboard, for example, and then using the shapes and textures produced as the starting point for a drawing or painting.

The people who saw the Surrealist pictures at the time were often shocked or surprised. Sometimes they laughed, and sometimes they got angry. We are harder to shock today; we see 'surreal' images everywhere – in comedy shows or in adverts. The original Surrealist pictures, however, can still be very disturbing.

'The art of Dalí [is] the most hallucinatory known.'

André Breton

▼ A Surrealist exhibition in Paris, 1938. The Surrealists loved to unsettle people. Here they have turned a gallery into a bedroom and a jungle!

To confuse and disturb

▲ Albert Einstein, c.1925. His ideas about time and space revolutionised the way people look at the world.

DALÍ AND EINSTEIN

Dalí was fascinated by the ideas of the scientist Albert Einstein (1879–1955). Einstein's theories about the nature of space and time changed the way people looked at the world. Before Einstein, people thought of the world as solid and constant. Einstein, however, suggested that everything was in flux. Even time, for instance, does not flow constantly but slows down or speeds up according to circumstances. Einstein's idea is known as the 'Theory of Relativity'.

Dalí was now an important member of the Surrealist group. He was even chosen to design the opening image of the *Second Surrealist Manifesto* published in 1930. In that year, Dalí and his lover, Gala Éluard, went to live in a cottage at Port Lligat, just outside Cadaqués. Here Dalí painted some of his most famous paintings, including *The Persistence of Memory*.

◀ Dalí and Gala's house at Port Lligat. Over the years, the couple transformed a fisherman's cottage into a large and beautiful home with a studio. Today the house is a museum devoted to Dalí and his work.

DOUBLE TAKE

At this time, Dalí was developing his own ideas about Surrealism and set them down in a book called *The Visible Woman* (1930). He felt that Surrealist artists should depict a kind of madness or fever in which a thing could look like one thing one moment and like another the next. Many of Dalí's paintings used these 'double' images to confuse and disturb people looking at them. For example, at the centre of *The Persistence of Memory* a watch flops over what looks like a strange, pale-coloured rock. If we look more closely, however, the rock could almost be a person, curled up on the sand.

TIMELINE ▶

January 1930	April 1930	Summer 1930	October 1930	December 1930	1931
De Rivera's rule in Spain ends, partly because of the economic depression.	*The Second Surrealist Manifesto* is published. Dalí designs its opening image.	Dalí and Gala buy and begin to restore a fisherman's cottage at Port Lligat, Cadaqués.	*L'Âge d'or*, a new Dalí-Buñuel film, opens in Paris. It is later banned after newspaper protests.	*The Visible Woman* is published.	Spain is declared a republic.

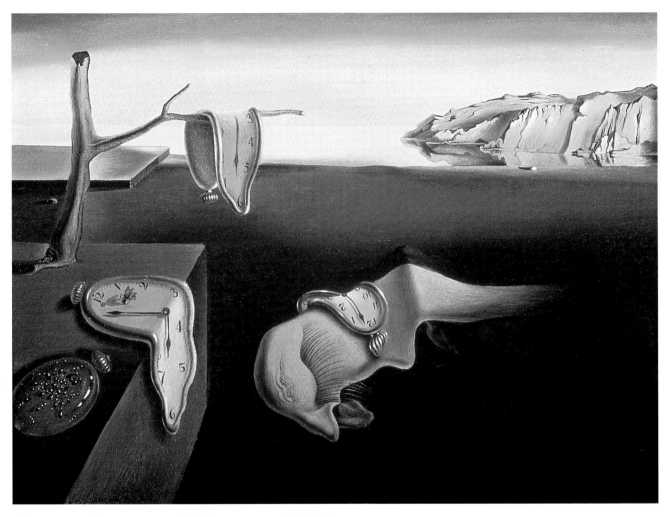

The Persistence of Memory, 1931

oil on canvas 24 x 33 cm The Museum of Modern Art, New York

Dalí called his paintings 'hand-painted dream photographs'. By this, he meant that the things he painted often look very real – like photographs – but at the same time are impossible or improbable – like dreams. Here he uses the technique to show watches melting on a hot beach. One watch hangs limply from a dead tree; another attracts a swarm of ants (see page 17). All the watches tell different times. The painting seems to portray just the kind of unstable, uncertain world Einstein proposed in his 'Theory of Relativity'.

'It will be possible to systematise confusion and contribute to the total discrediting of the world of reality.'

Salvador Dalí on using double imagery, The Visible Woman

Love and marriage

In 1934, Dalí finally married Gala. She had been his muse and great love ever since they had met in 1929. At the time, Gala was already married to the Surrealist poet Paul Éluard (1895-1952). Dalí's father was so angered by their relationship that he threw Dalí out of the family home. In protest, Dalí shaved off his hair.

Dalí adored Gala. She had helped him recover from a deep depression he had suffered from before they met and he often used her as a model. They spent most of their time happily at Port Lligat.

Dalí's success continued. Shortly after his marriage he had his first London exhibition. A little later the couple travelled to New York, where they received a lot of flattering attention.

▲ *The Angelus*, Jean-François Millet, 1857-59. The Angelus is a Christian prayer said at morning, noon and evening.

▲ Dalí poses Gala for one of his paintings at Port Lligat. He thought the shape of her back and hips was that of the perfect female.

THE ANGELUS OF GALA

Dalí painted this portrait of Gala a few years after they first met. He shows her from both the front and back, just as if she were looking in a mirror. There is no mirror to be seen, though, and there are some odd differences between the two Galas. While one of them is sitting on a box, the other is perched on a wheelbarrow!

In the background is a picture of two farm workers praying in a field at dusk. Dalí based the picture on a popular painting called *The Angelus* by the 19th-century French artist Jean-François Millet (1814-75). A copy of the painting had hung in Dalí's first school and haunted Dalí throughout his life.

TIMELINE ▶

January 1933	November 1933	1934	January 1934	October 1934	November 1934
Nazi party comes to power in Germany, under leader Adolf Hitler.	Dalí has his first solo exhibition in the United States at the Julien Levy Gallery, New York.	Dalí quarrels with André Breton. Begins to move away from the Surrealist group.	Dalí marries Gala.	Dalí has his first solo exhibition in Britain, at the Zwemmer Gallery, London.	Dalí and Gala visit New York for the first time.

The Angelus of Gala, 1935

oil on panel 32 x 27 cm Museum of Modern Art, New York

Dalí leaves us unsure whether it is Gala who is praying or whether the painting is itself a kind of prayer to his wife. Whatever we decide, the picture shows Dalí's deep devotion to Gala. As in many of his pictures, Dalí painted this portrait in a painstaking way, paying a lot of attention to detail. Gala's beautiful embroidered jacket, for example, could almost be real.

The Spanish Civil War

While Dalí was enjoying his international success, the situation in Spain was less happy. From 1936 to 1939, a bloody civil war raged in Spain. The Spanish Civil War was fought between those who believed that Spain should be a monarchy – that is, ruled by a king – and those who thought it should be a republic led by an elected president. Many republicans were ordinary workers or the supporters of left-wing parties such as the socialists and communists. The monarchists, by contrast, were often landowners and business people, or members of the army or the Roman Catholic Church.

A NEW REPUBLIC

For hundreds of years, Spain had been a monarchy. In 1931, however, the Spanish people voted for their country to become a republic. The new government carried out wide-ranging reforms. It shared out farmland and gave regions like Catalonia more independence.

▲ *Aidez l'Espagne*, Joan Miró, 1937
The Catalan painter Joan Miró was a passionate supporter of the Republicans. This poster calls on the French to 'Help Spain' and fight against Franco.

AN END TO REFORMS

Increasingly, however, many Spanish people came to believe that the reforms were too extreme. In 1933, a new government came to power and brought an end to the reforms. In some parts of Spain, workers rebelled against the government. In Barcelona, for example, workers declared Catalonia an independent republic. Government soldiers brutally put down the revolts, killing more than a thousand people.

◀ The Nationalist leader, General Franco, was ruthless in his determination to overthrow the elected Republican government.

▲ Civilians defend a makeshift barricade in Barcelona, 1937. Most people in Barcelona supported the Republican cause.

In 1936, the Spanish president called another election. This time, the left-wing republican parties won by a small number of votes. Almost at once, however, a monarchist rebellion broke out. The rebels, led by General Francisco Franco (1892-1975), soon gained control of about a third of Spain. The rebels were known as Nationalists. The forces who defended the republic were called Loyalists or Republicans.

FOREIGN INTERVENTION

Neither side was strong enough to win the war quickly, and sought help from abroad. Hitler's Nazi Germany and Fascist Italy, ruled by Mussolini, sent tanks, planes and soldiers to help the Nationalists. The communist Soviet Union sent military aid to the Republicans. In addition, thousands of volunteers came from all over the world to help the Republican cause.

Altogether more than 500,000 Spaniards died as a result of the war. Many of these were civilians (non-soldiers), who were killed when their towns and cities were bombed or died due to lack of food. Eventually, in March 1939 the Nationalists defeated the Republicans and General Franco established a dictatorship.

He was to remain in power for over 35 years.

TAKING SIDES

During the Spanish Civil War, most Spanish artists, including Pablo Picasso and Joan Miró, supported the Republicans. In 1937, for example, Picasso produced a huge painting to commemorate the Spanish town of Guernica, which had been bombed by German planes. The Surrealists, too, were in general pro-Republican. Dalí, however, steadfastly refused to support either side, even after Nationalists executed his friend the poet Lorca in 1936.

The horror of war

▲ The brushstrokes in this close-up of *Autumn Cannibalism* are invisible.

IN DETAIL

Dalí created his paintings with a lot of care. Many artists at this time painted very freely, using big, bold brushstrokes that are visible in their paintings. By contrast, Dalí painted so that we are unable to see a single brushstroke, making his pictures appear smooth and glossy. This way of painting was sometimes called 'academic' and was very popular in the 19th century.

Dalí used the academic style to make the strangest things seem real. You can almost feel and even smell them – and not just see them! In the detail of *Autumn Cannibalism* above, it is hard not to shudder as you watch the shining metal knife slice into the soft, caramel-coloured flesh.

Although Dalí did not take sides in the Spanish Civil War, he was horrified by the destruction it caused. He painted *Autumn Cannibalism* soon after the outbreak of the war. In this famous painting, two monstrous human beings dine off each other's bodies. The first man scoops out a spoonful of the second man's flesh, while the second man slices into the first man's skin.

A SPANISH TRADITION

Dalí was not the first Spanish artist to try to convey the horror of war. In the early 19th century, the Spanish artist Francisco Goya was moved to paint by another period of war in Spain's history and produced many pictures on the subject. In *The Colossus* (below), Goya showed a fierce giant spreading fear and panic among hundreds of people. Many experts think that Goya's 'colossus' – or giant figure – is a symbol of war. In another picture, he depicted the giant Saturn eating his own child. Like Dalí, he uses cannibalism to show his disgust of war.

▲ *The Colossus*, Francisco Goya, c. 1810. Many artists have tried to show the pointless destruction caused by war. Goya painted this after the troops of the French emperor Napoleon invaded Spain in 1809.

Autumn Cannibalism, 1936

oil on canvas 65 x 65 cm Tate Modern, London

This gruesome painting uses mostly gloomy colours – chocolate browns and milky greys. Even the sky is grey and empty, except for a looming storm cloud. Drawers, like the one bottom right, featured in many of Dalí's pictures about this time – he saw them both as a symbol of the hidden unconscious and also as a source of bad smells, in this case the smell of war.

'From all parts of martyred Spain rose a smell … of burned curates' fat and of quartered spiritual flesh that mingled with the smell of … death.'

Salvador Dalí

Star of the show

DALÍ AND DESIGN

From the 1930s, Dalí spent a lot of his time designing Surrealist objects as well as painting. Some critics even think that Dalí was a better designer than painter! He was particularly interested in fashion and he designed extravagant jewellery and clothes. He worked closely with Italian designer Elsa Schiaparelli (1890-1973). They created a women's suit with pockets that looked like drawers, as well as a dress with a pattern of lobsters, parsley and mayonnaise.

▶ Dalí and Elsa Schiaparelli's lobster dress.

▲ Dalí in his diving suit with other Surrealist painters and writers in London in 1936.

Despite the civil war, Dalí continued to travel and his international reputation reached new heights. In 1936, there was an exhibition of Surrealist art in London. Dalí was the star of the show. He attracted a lot of attention from the press, especially when he gave a lecture at the gallery while wearing a diving suit! Some Surrealist artists, especially Breton, criticised Dalí for seeking fame. Breton was a communist, and he also accused Dalí of supporting right-wing extremists such as the German dictator, Adolf Hitler.

SURREALIST FURNITURE

At this time, Dalí became friends with an English millionaire named Edward James. From 1936 to 1939 James gave Dalí a monthly income in return for all his paintings and drawings. Dalí also created Surrealist pieces of furniture for James, including a pink sofa in the form of lips, a telephone with a lobster instead of a receiver, and a chair with hands.

TIMELINE ▶

June 1936	July 1936	August 1936	December 1936	December 1936
The International Surrealist Exhibition opens in London. Dalí lectures at it dressed in a diving suit.	The Spanish Civil War begins.	Lorca is shot dead by Nationalists.	Dalí signs contract with Edward James ensuring a monthly income for next 3 years.	Dalí appears on the front cover of the US magazine *Time*.

Lobster Telephone, 1936
telephone with painted plaster lobster 15 x 30 x 17 cm Tate Modern, London

Imagine answering a telephone like this! Dalí's sense of the absurd and ridiculous is particularly apparent in 'Surrealist' objects like this one. There is always an air of menace behind his jokes, though.

'It is not necessary for the public to know whether I am joking or whether I am serious, just as it is not necessary for me to know it myself.'

Salvador Dalí

Painting the unconscious mind

In 1938, Dalí went to visit the famous thinker Sigmund Freud in London and drew several pictures of him. He also showed him his painting *The Metamorphosis of Narcissus*.

ROMAN MYTH

The ancient Roman writer Ovid told a story about a handsome young man named Narcissus. Looking into a pool, Narcissus fell so in love with his own reflection that he was unable to move. Eventually, he died and the gods changed him into a spring flower – the narcissus.

▲ *Echo and Narcissus*, Nicolas Poussin, 1627-28. Many artists have painted the story of Narcissus. In this version by the 17th-century French painter Poussin, Narcissus lies dead as narcissus flowers sprout from his head.

DALÍ AND FREUD

Freud's ideas about the human personality were a powerful influence on Dalí's work and the Surrealists as a whole (see page 18). Freud described a condition in which a person becomes so obsessed with himself that he is unable to love anyone else. Freud called this condition narcissism, after the legendary Narcissus. Freud often used characters in ancient myth to describe particular psychological types – another example is the 'Oedipus complex', a condition where a man is obsessed with his mother. Oedipus was a character from ancient Greek myth who mistakenly married his mother.

In Dalí's painting, we can see Narcissus both before and after his metamorphosis (change). On the left, Narcissus kneels over a pool. On the right, both his body and reflection have turned to stone. His head has become an egg, out of which bursts a white flower. There is even another Narcissus in the painting, similar to the others – can you see where?

TIMELINE ▶

January 1937	June 1937	July 1937	January 1938	March 1938	July 1938
Dalí travels to Hollywood and meets the Marx brothers.	Picasso shows *Guernica*, his famous anti-war picture.	Dalí paints *The Metamorphosis of Narcissus* and writes a poem of the same name.	International Surrealists Exhibition opens in Paris. Dalí takes part in it.	Hitler makes Austria part of Germany. Breton and Surrealists condemn Dalí's comments on Hitler.	Dalí meets Freud in London.

The Metamorphosis of Narcissus, 1937
oil on canvas 51x 78 cm Tate Modern, London

In his painting, Dalí shows how the self-love of narcissism can lead to death and decay. He also suggests, however, that narcissism is not all negative, that it may create beautiful things, like the springtime flower. The story of Narcissus fascinated Dalí. He even wrote a long poem about it at the same time as he was working on this painting.

'They ... scent out the countless narcissistic smells
that waft out of all our drawers.'

Salvador Dalí on Freud's theories

The power of Hitler

▲ Hitler stands next to Chamberlain (second from right) after signing the Munich Pact in September 1938.

LOOMING WAR

In 1938, Britain's prime minister, Neville Chamberlain (1869-1940), went to Munich to meet Hitler, hoping to avoid war. Britain's policy was known as 'Appeasement'. At the meeting, Hitler and Chamberlain agreed that Germany could take over the Sudetenland, which was part of Czechoslovakia. Chamberlain returned to Britain claiming he brought 'peace in our time'. Dalí painted *The Enigma of Hitler* soon after this event, unconvinced by the agreement. History proved him right. By March 1939, Hitler's armies had taken over all of Czechoslovakia.

In 1938, the German dictator, Adolf Hitler, sent troops into the neighbouring country of Austria. He had never tried to hide the fact that he wanted to build a mighty German empire and aggressively pursued his aims. Other European countries tried to keep the peace (see panel), and let Hitler take part of Czechoslovakia (the modern Czech Republic and Slovakia), too.

Dalí was fascinated by Hitler's power and charisma, although he did not always admire his beliefs. Many of the other Surrealists were communists and opposed Hitler whole-heartedly. They accused Dalí of supporting Hitler, and eventually expelled him from the group.

EUROPE AT WAR

In September 1939, German troops invaded Poland and Britain declared war on Germany. The Second World War had begun. At the time, Dalí and Gala were in Paris. At first, they moved to southwest France, far away from any possible fighting. In 1940, however, Germany invaded and occupied France. Dalí and Gala, along with many other writers and artists, decided to leave for the safe haven of the United States.

▲ Dalí stands on deck as his ship arrives in New York, 1936. During this trip, he received a lot of press attention. At the end of the year, he even appeared on the cover of the popular *Time* magazine. When Dalí returned to the city in 1940, he was already a celebrity there.

TIMELINE ▶

September 1938	Early 1939	September 1939	June 1940	August 1940	November 1941	December 1941	October 1942
Chamberlain meets Hitler in Munich.	Surrealist group expels Dalí. Spanish Civil War ends.	World War II begins. Spain remains neutral.	Germany occupies France.	Dalí and Gala escape to the United States.	Dalí and Miró joint exhibition at the Museum of Modern Art, New York.	The United States enters war after Japan bombs Pearl Harbor.	Dalí publishes his autobiography, *The Secret Life of Salvador Dalí*.

The Enigma of Hitler, 1939

oil on canvas 51.2 x 79.3 cm Museo Nacional Central de Arte Reina Sofía, Madrid, Spain

The Enigma of Hitler is full of gloom and the threat of war. A photograph of Hitler, torn out of a newspaper, lies on a plate. One end of a giant black telephone receiver is turning into a lobster claw, showing how war is breaking out, despite all the talk. Before World War II, no one was quite sure what Hitler would do next – this is the enigma, or 'mystery', of the title.

'If Hitler were to ever conquer Europe, he would do away with hysterics of my kind... Hitler interested me purely as a focus for my own mania and because he struck me as having an unequalled disaster value.'

Salvador Dalí

Dalí in the United States

▲ New York's famous Manhattan skyline in the 1940s seemed to sum up America's glamorous image.

In the mid-1930s, the United States was emerging from the years of depression that had followed the Wall Street Crash of 1929. To many Europeans, it seemed once again a country full of energy and hope, as it had done at the start of the 20th century. They were excited by American music, by the dizzying skyscrapers of America's bustling cities, and by Hollywood movies and their glamorous stars. Everything about Europe, by contrast, seemed tired and old-fashioned.

LIVING THE AMERICAN DREAM

During his visits to the United States in the 1930s, Dalí had fallen in love with the country. When he and Gala went to live there in 1940, they were already well known and had a wide circle of friends. They lived at the house of a rich American woman named Caresse Crosby in the state of Virginia. Dalí was much sought after by high-society hostesses and journalists and had plenty of offers of work.

A SECRET LIFE

American magazines particularly liked to report on Dalí's eccentric lifestyle. One report called 'Dalí's Daffy Day' included a picture of the painter at work, sitting on a chair balanced on four turtles. Dalí also attracted attention in 1942 when he published his autobiography – *The Secret Life of Salvador Dalí*. The book is full of fantastic stories about Dalí's early life. Some of the stories are true; others Dalí made up. He believed that, like fake jewels, false memories were 'the most real, the most brilliant'.

IN THE MONEY

In the United States, Dalí made a lot of money by painting portraits of famous people and designing advertisements. André Breton accused Dalí of being greedy, and joked that he was 'Avida Dollars', that is, 'mad about dollars'. (Avida Dollars is an anagram of the name Salvador Dalí.)

Dalí also went to work in Hollywood. He helped the director Alfred Hitchcock (1889-1980) make his thriller *Spellbound* (1945). In the film, a psychiatrist solves a murder by analysing her patient's dreams. Dalí designed the film sets used to represent the man's dreams.

▲ *The Moon, Woman Cuts the Circle*, Jackson Pollock, c. 1943. Jackson Pollock was one of a new generation of American artists who were taking art in radical and exciting directions. As a result, New York was replacing Paris as the centre of the art world.

▲ A scene designed by Dalí for the dream sequences of Hitchcock's *Spellbound*. Alfred Hitchcock was one of the leading film directors of the time and it says much for Dalí's status as a popular artist that he was invited to work with him.

THE ATOMIC AGE

In 1941, Germany's ally Japan bombed Pearl Harbor, a US naval base in Hawaii, and the United States entered the war on the side of Britain. The war came to an end in 1945, soon after a US plane dropped the first atomic bomb on Hiroshima in Japan, killing 240,000 people. This terrible explosion filled Dalí with wonder rather than horror. He wrote that the explosion of an atomic bomb reminded him of 'mossy and mushroomy trees of an earthly paradise'.

The man with the moustache

▲ Dalí in his studio at Port Lligat in the 1950s. A cross hangs on the wall above him.

MYSTICAL EXPERIENCES

Dalí was brought up in a strongly Roman Catholic country. Although Dalí's father did not believe in a god, his mother was very pious. Nevertheless, until the 1940s, Dalí paid little attention to religion in his work, except sometimes to poke fun at it. After World War II, however, he became drawn to religion and in particular to mysticism. A mystic has religious experiences such as visions that bring him or her into direct contact with God. Dalí saw such experiences as Surrealist because they seemed to belong to the world of the imagination and the unconscious mind.

Dalí's later work includes many religious paintings. These pictures are very unusual and some people have questioned the sincerity of Dalí's belief. Others have found his religious work profoundly moving.

Dalí and Gala did not return to Europe until 1949. For the rest of his life, Dalí would be an international star – as famous for his long, curly moustache and walking stick as for his paintings. He loved to appear on television, and he wrote more books full of stories about his life. In 1954, he even published a book about his own moustache!

> *'I shall use my work to show the unity of the universe, by showing the spirituality of all substance.'*
>
> *Salvador Dalí*

TURNING TO RELIGION

Dalí and Gala divided their time between Paris, New York and Port Lligat, enjoying a life of luxury. Only at Port Lligat did Dalí really have the time to paint. After the war, many of his paintings were about religion (see panel). In 1955, Dalí visited the Pope and, in 1958, he and Gala were married again in church.

◀ Salvador Dalí in front of one of his paintings in 1957. As usual he carries a walking stick. He also wears a Catalan cap or *barretina* (see page 9).

TIMELINE ▶

1945	August 1945	1949	1954	1955	1958	1961
Dalí works with director Alfred Hitchcock on the film *Spellbound*.	The United States drops the first atomic bomb on Hiroshima, Japan.	Dalí and Gala return to Europe.	*Dalí's Moustache* is published.	Dali meets the Pope.	Dalí marries Gala in church.	The Soviet Union puts the first human into space.

Christ of St John of the Cross, 1951
oil on canvas 205 x 116 cm St Mungo Museum of Religious Art and Life, Glasgow

The inspiration for this painting came from the vision of a 16th-century preacher called Saint John of the Cross. In the vision, the preacher saw Christ from above, as if from heaven. In Dalí's painting of the vision, the viewer seems to be floating in the air, gazing down on the cross from a dizzying height.

The final performance

THE THEATRE-MUSEUM

In 1960, the mayor of Figueres asked Dalí to donate one of his paintings to the town museum. Dalí refused. Instead, he promised to build a whole museum! The Theatre-Museum, as it was called, opened in 1974, when Dalí was 70 years old.

From outside the museum looks very different from most art museums. The walls are bright pink, and on the roof are rows of huge eggs. Inside, the museum is just as strange. For example, in one room, there is a bed with fish for its feet. Standing next to the bed is the skeleton of a gorilla, painted gold.

▲ Outside the Theatre-Museum, Figueres. The building itself is a great Surrealist work of art.

▲ Dalí holds up a picture of Gala. The photograph was taken after her death in 1982. Dalí never really recovered from the loss of his beloved wife.

Even as he grew older, Dalí continued to be interested in the world around him. He was fascinated, for example, by developments in physics and genetics and incorporated these interests into his art. He began to paint using an optical instrument called a Wheatstone stereoscope (see right). Stereoscopy is the science of how the human eye sees in three dimensions rather than just two. Dalí thought of the gift of sight as something spiritual and almost miraculous.

LAST YEARS OF GRIEF

Dalí carried on a life in the media spotlight. In 1964, he published a second autobiography, which he half-jokingly, half-boastfully called *My Life as a Genius*. In 1982, however, Gala died and Dalí was so grief-stricken that he, too, became ill. Thereafter he lived his life in virtual seclusion, cared for by nurses. He died in 1989 and was buried beneath the Theatre-Museum in Figueres.

TIMELINE ▶

1964	1974	1975	1982	June 1982	July 1982	1983	1989
Dalí's second autobiography, *My Life as a Genius*, is published.	The Theatre-Museum opens in Figueres.	Franco dies. Spain becomes a democratic country headed by a monarch.	The Salvador Dalí Museum opens in St Petersburg, Florida.	Gala dies.	The Spanish king, Juan Carlos, gives Dalí the title of Marquis of Púbol.	Dalí finishes his last painting, *The Swallow's Tail*.	Dalí dies at Figueres on 23 January.

Dalí from the Back Painting Gala from the Back Externalised by Six Virtual Corneas Provisionally Reflected in Six Real Mirrors (unfinished), 1972–73

oil on canvas (one section of two) 60 x 60 cm Gala-Salvador Dalí Foundation, Figueres, Spain

Dalí's later paintings are sometimes very complicated. In this work, he used a stereoscope to give the viewer the sensation of looking into a real space and not just onto a flat canvas. Here there are multiple layers of 'real' space – from the painting itself to the mirror and the landscape outside the window. We are looking at Dalí painting Gala watching Dalí, who looks back at her – and us – out of the mirror!

'The most extraordinary being you could possibly encounter, the superstar...'

Salvador Dalí on Gala

Dalí's legacy

Salvador Dalí is one of the most popular modern painters. His paintings and objects are still able to surprise and shock us, or even make us laugh. Although many of the themes Dalí treated in his art are very serious, he always wanted his paintings to entertain the people looking at them. Because of this, some critics think of Dalí as a kind of showman or as a magician performing conjuring tricks.

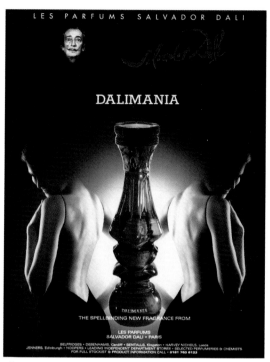

DALIMANIA

▲ Dalí enjoyed being famous and was happy to make money out of his fame. This perfume bearing his name was launched in 1983.

REACT TO THE IMAGE

Many people find modern artists difficult to understand. Dalí, however, tried to appeal to people in a simple and direct way. In fact, he didn't want people to understand his paintings at all, but to react to them – just as if they were their own dreams. Everyone would shiver if they saw a swarm of ants on their hand. Everyone is puzzled and disturbed when they see something that is normally solid melting – like the watches on the beach.

Enter a new world of long-lasting power...

▲ Dalí's popular appeal has meant Surrealist images have entered our everyday life, through television and advertising.

'The secret of my influence has always been that it remained secret.'

Salvador Dalí

40

POP ART

Dalí's directness, sense of fun and popular appeal are his most important legacies to modern art. Many artists working today want to make art not just for a small band of experts but for a wide audience made up of all sorts of people. This was one of the aims of the Pop artists, who worked during the 1960s and early 1970s. The most famous Pop artist is Andy Warhol (1928-87). Warhol used popular images from newspapers, film, TV, and even everyday products like soup cans to create entertaining artworks.

▲ Like Dalí, Damien Hirst has become famous for shocking us.

ARTIST AS SHOWMAN

Damien Hirst (b.1966) is a modern British artist who has learned a great deal from Dalí. Hirst is not really a painter or a sculptor. Like Dalí, he is a showman – a conjurer of surprising and shocking objects. Some of his most famous works have consisted of dead animals such as cows and sharks sliced in half and displayed in cases. Naturally enough, we are revolted and upset by such sights. However, Hirst's – like Dalí's – artworks can also lead us to ponder serious subjects such as death and decay – the very same subjects artists have been dealing with for hundreds of years.

◀ Pop artist Andy Warhol developed Dalí's ideas about how ordinary, everyday objects could be made extraordinary. Warhol, like Dalí, also became famous for his appearance!

Two Catalan Surrealists

Dalí was not the only Surrealist painter from Catalonia. Joan Miró (1893-1983) came from there too. To begin with, the two artists were friendly and admired each other's paintings. Slightly older than Dalí, Miró encouraged the young artist to broaden his horizons. In 1929, in Paris Miró introduced Dalí to the Surrealists. Over the years, the two artists' work developed in very different directions (see Miró's work on pages 18 and 24).

You are without doubt a very gifted man with a brilliant career ahead of you – in Paris!

▲ After visiting Dalí's studio in Figueres in 1927, Miró wrote to him, encouraging him to come to Paris to further his career.

Miró returns the line, dot ... and colours to their pure, elemental, magical possibilities... Miró's art is too big for the stupid world of our artists and intellectuals.

◄ Dalí was enthusiastic about Miró's work, too. He wrote this in a review of an exhibition of Miró's paintings in 1928.

JOAN MIRÓ

Joan Miró grew up on a farm near Barcelona and was very proud of being Catalan. His paintings often include Catalan symbols such as the *barettina*. Even after he moved to Paris in 1919, he always spent the summers on his father's farm.

Miró was one of the first artists to join the Surrealist group. He signed the first *Surrealist Manifesto*, and remained committed to the group's ideals. Like the other Surrealists, Miró used his art to explore the unconscious mind. During his early career, he lived in great poverty and near starvation. He even wrote that one of his paintings was inspired 'by my hallucinations brought on by hunger'. Miró loved music and poetry, and tried to capture their qualities in his art.

► Miró working on a painting, 1967.

TIMELINE ►

1904	1921	1924	1928	1930
11 May 1904 Salvador Dalí Domènech is born in Figueres, Catalonia, Spain.	**October 1921** Goes to the San Fernando Academy of Fine Art, Madrid.	**May 1924** Serves a one-month prison sentence.	**March 1928** Publishes the *Yellow Manifesto*.	**January 1930** De Rivera dictatorship ends.
1908 Sister, Ana Mariá, is born.	**1922** The Surrealist group forms in Paris.	**October 1924** *Surrealist Manifesto* published.	**April 1929** Makes film *Un chien andalou* with Buñuel.	**April 1930** Designs frontispiece of *The Second Surrealist Manifesto*.
1914 Gaudí's Guell Park opens in Barcelona.	**1923** Sigmund Freud's *The Interpretation of Dreams* is published in Spanish.	**November 1925** First solo exhibition held in Barcelona.	**Summer 1929** Begins affair with Gala Éluard.	**Summer 1930** Buys home Port Lligat, Cadaqués.
1914-1918 World War I.	**September 1923** De Rivero dictatorship in Spain.	**April 1926** First trip to Paris; visits Picasso and Miró.	**October 1929** *Un chien andalou* opens in Paris. The Wall Street Crash.	**October 1930** *L'Âge d'or*, a new Dalí-Buñuel film, opens in Paris.
1917 Holds an exhibition in the family apartment.	**October 1923** Suspended by the Academy.	**October 1926** Expelled from the Academy.	**November 1929** Has his first exhibition in Paris.	**December 1930** *The Visible Woman* is published.
February 1921 Mother dies.		**January 1927** Dalí has his second one-man show.		

CONTRASTING PERSONALITIES

The two artists' personalities were very different too. Miró was very modest and disliked appearing in public. He thought that Dalí was too eager to be famous. When Dalí began to design clothes, Miró accused him of being a 'painter of neckties'. The two men also had opposing political views. During the Spanish Civil War, Miró supported the Republicans, whereas Dalí refused to take sides (see page 25).

The spectacle of the sky overwhelms me. I'm overwhelmed when I see, in an immense sky, the crescent of the moon, or the sun. It is there, in my pictures: tiny forms in huge empty spaces. Empty spaces, empty horizons, empty plains …

▲ Miró points to the inspiration behind his art.

▶ Dalí was always much more arrogant than Miró. He seemed to find inspiration in himself! He loved being famous. ▼

The only difference between me and the Surrealists is that I am a Surrealist.

Every morning when I awake the greatest of joys is mine – that of being Salvador Dalí.

Miró was the very incarnation of freedom. His art was airier, freer, lighter than anything I had seen before.

◀ Dalí and Miró attracted very different admirers. The Swiss Surrealist sculptor Alberto Giacometti (1901-66) was a close friend of Miró and wrote this about his art.

▶ U.S. artist Andy Warhol got to know Dalí and Gala in the 1960s. Warhol did not seem particularly interested in Dalí's art. He liked Dalí above all because he was a star!

It's like being with royalty or circus people. That's why I like being with Dalí – because it's not like being with an artist…

1931	1934	1938	1942	1964
1931 Spain is declared a republic.	**November 1934** Visits New York for the first time.	**March 1938** Hitler makes Austria part of Germany.	**October 1942** *The Secret Life of Salvador Dalí* is published.	**1964** *My Life as a Genius* is published.
January 1933 Adolf Hitler gains power in Germany.	**June 1936** Attends International Surrealist Exhibition in London.	**July 1938** Meets Freud.	**1945** Works on the film *Spellbound*.	**1974** The Theatre-Museum opens in Figueres.
November 1933 First solo exhibition in the USA.	**1936-39** The Spanish Civil War.	**Early 1939** Expelled from Surrealist group.	**1949** Returns to Europe.	**1975** Franco dies. Spain becomes a democracy.
January 1934 Marries Gala.	**December 1936** On the front cover of *Time*.	**1939-45** World War II.	**1954** *Dalí's Moustache* is published.	**June 1982** Gala dies.
1934 Moving away from the Surrealist group.	**January 1938** Takes part in International Surrealists Exhibition in Paris.	**August 1940** Goes to the United States.	**1955** Meets the Pope.	**1983** Finishes last painting, *The Swallow's Tail*.
Ocotober 1934 First solo exhibition in Britain.		**November 1941** Has joint exhibition with Miró at the Museum of Modern Art, New York.	**1958** Marries Gala in church.	**1989** Dalí dies at Figueres on 23 January.

Glossary

anarchism: the belief that people should be able to live their lives free of church or government laws.

avant-garde: describes new, experimental or radical ideas. From the French for vanguard, the first troops into battle.

collage: a picture made by pasting photographs, newspaper cuttings, string, labels and other objects on to a flat surface.

communism: a political system first suggested by Karl Marx (1818-83) under which every one shares a country's goods and property.

Cubism: the name of an art movement evolving in Paris in about 1907 led by Pablo Picasso (1881-1973) and Georges Braque (1882-1963). The Cubists painted multiple angles of a person or object so they were all seen at once.

dictator: a ruler who has total control over a country.

empire: a large number of countries ruled by a more powerful country.

enigma: a mystery.

Expressionism: an approach to painting which communicates an emotional state of mind rather than external reality. The Norwegian artist Edvard Munch (1863-1944), who painted *The Scream*, was a leading Expressionist.

fascist: describes an extreme right-wing political system where government has total power, usually focused around a charismatic leader.

frottage: using rubbings of a surface to obtain a textured effect.

genetics: the study of genes, the parts of living cells that are duplicated from one generation to the next and determine heredity.

hallucination: something which the mind sees or experiences but which does not exist in reality.

Impressionists: a group of artists based in Paris during the late nineteenth century who painted 'impressions' of the world with broad brushstrokes of pure, unmixed colour. The group included Auguste Renoir (1841-1919), Claude Monet (1840-1926) and Edgar Degas (1834-1917).

left-wing: adjective used to describe socialist or communist political views.

manifesto: a declaration of beliefs.

monarchy: a system of government headed by a king or queen.

montage: a method of editing film so that the picture cuts quickly from one image to another.

mysticism: a devout form of religious belief where a person has direct contact with God through spiritual experiences such as visions.

Nazi: anything to do with the National Socialist German Workers' Party, the extreme right-wing political party led by Adolf Hitler that ruled Germany between 1933 and 1945.

Old Masters: the name used to describe the greatest European painters from around 1500-1800, including Leonardo da Vinci (1452-1519), Michelangelo (1475-1564), Velázquez (1599-1660) and Jan Vermeer (1632-75).

Pop art: the art movement that emerged in the United States in the 1960s which sought to make art more popular by featuring everyday objects, famous people or well-known designs. Andy Warhol (1928-87) was one of the most famous Pop artists.

republic: a system of government headed by an elected president.

right-wing: adjective used to describe conservative or traditionalist political views.

Roman Catholicism: one of the major Christian churches; the leader of the Roman Catholic Church is the Pope, who lives in the Vatican City in Rome.

socialism: a political system in which the government tries to make sure that everyone has a fair income and equal rights.

Surrealism: an intellectual movement that emerged in the 1920s that tried to depict the life of our unconscious minds and dreams. The Surrealists included artists, writers and film-makers.

unconscious: describes the part of a person's mind that lies outside the conscious mind we use in everyday waking life. Dreams and the imagination are expressions of the unconscious.

Museums and galleries

Works by Dalí are exhibited in museums and galleries all around the world. Some of the ones listed here are devoted solely to Dalí, but most have a wide range of other artists' works on display.

Even if you can't visit any of these galleries yourself, you may be able to visit their websites. Gallery websites often show pictures of the artworks they have on display. Some of the websites even offer virtual tours which allow you to wander around and look at different paintings while sitting comfortably in front of your computer! Most of the international websites detailed below include an option that allows you to view them in English.

Dalí Universe, London
County Hall,
Riverside Building,
London SE1 7PB
www.daliuniverse.com

Fundació Gala-Salvador Dalí
This organisation runs three Dalí museums in Spain (listed below). Their website connects to all three museums.
www.dali-estate.org

Dalí Theatre-Museum
Plaça Gala i Salvador Dalí, s/s
17600 Figueres
Spain

Gala-Dalí Castle Museum-House, Spain
Casa-Museu Castell Gala Dalí
Púbol
17120 la Pera
Spain

Salvador Dalí Museum-House
Port Lligat
Cadaqués
Spain

Salvador Dalí Art Gallery
A virtual art gallery featuring 1500 of Dalí's works
www.dali-gallery.com

Salvador Dalí Museum, St Petersburg
1000 Third Street South
St Petersburg
Florida 33701-4901
USA
www.salvadordalimuseum.org

Museum of Modern Art, New York
11 West 53 Street
New York
NY 10019-5497
USA
www.moma.org

Museo Nacional Centro de Arte Reina Sofía
Plaza Santa Isabel, 52
28012 Madrid
Spain
www.museoreinasofia.es

National Gallery of Australia
Parkes Place
Parkes
ACT 2600
Australia
www.nga.gov.au

Tate Modern, London
Bankside
London SE1 9TG
www.tate.org.uk/modern

Index

anarchism 8, 44
The Angelus (Millet) 22
The Angelus of Gala 23
ants 16, 17, 27, 40
atomic bomb 35, 36
Autumn Cannibalism 26-27

Barcelona 6, 7, 8-9, 24, 25
barretina (hat) 9, 36, 42
Bonaparte, Napoleon 6
Breton, André 10, 12, 18, 28, 30
Buñuel, Luis 10, 11, 16-17

Cadaqués 7, 20
Catalonia 6, 8, 9, 24, 42
Chamberlain, Neville 32
Un chien andalou (film by Dalí and
Buñuel) 16-17, 18
    still from 17
Chirico, Giorgio de 10
Christ of St John of the Cross 36
collage 18, 44
The Colossus (Goya) 26
communism 8, 10, 25, 28, 44
Crosby, Caresse 34
Cubism 8, 10, 11, 44

Dalí, Ana Mariá (sister) 6, 7, 8,
    14, 15
Dalí, Felipa (mother) 6, 7, 10
Dalí, Gala (wife) 16, 20, 22-23,
    32, 38-39
Dalí, Salvador (father) 6-9, 16, 22
Dalí, Salvador
    appearance of 10, 22, 36, 41
    autobiographies of 7, 34, 38
    colour, use of 9, 11, 27
    and design 28
    education 6, 10
    and fashion 28, 40, 43
    influences on 6-9, 10, 14, 16,
        26, 36
    photographs of 6, 7, 12, 14, 22,
        28, 32, 36, 38
    portraits by 9, 11, 13, 23, 39
    and religion 36-37
    and science 20, 38
    style of art 9, 10, 21, 23, 26
    writings of 31, 34, 36, 38

Dalí from the Back Painting Gala…
    39
Dialogue of Insects (Miró) 18
double images 20, 21
dreams 16, 18, 35

Echo and Narcissus (Poussin) 30
Einstein, Albert 20, 21
Eisenstein, Sergei 16
Éluard, Gala *See* Dalí, Gala
Éluard, Paul 22
The Enigma of Hitler 33
Expressionism 10, 44

Figueres 6, 7, 14, 38
film-making 16-17, 20, 35
Franco, Francisco (General) 24,
    25, 38
Freud, Sigmund 10, 18, 30
frottage 18, 44

Gaudí, Antonio 8
Goya, Francisco de 10, 26

Hirst, Damien 41
Hitchcock, Alfred 35, 36
Hitler, Adolf 22, 25, 28, 30, 32, 33
Hollywood 30, 35

Impressionism 9, 44

James, Edward 28

The Lacemaker (Vermeer) 14
lobsters 28, 29, 31
Lobster Telephone 29
London 22, 28, 30
Lorca, Federico García 10, 12-13,
    14, 25, 28

Marx, Karl 8
Matisse, Henri 19
Melancholy: The Street
    (de Chirico) 10
The Metamorphosis of Narcissus 30-31
Millet, Jean-François 22
Miró, Joan 12, 14, 18, 24, 25, 32,
    42-43
montage 16, 44

mysticism 36, 44

narcissism 30
Narcissus, legend of 30

Old Masters 14, 22, 26, 30, 44

Paris 8, 12, 14, 16, 30, 32, 35
The Persistence of Memory 20-21
Picasso, Pablo 8, 12, 13, 14, 25, 30
Pierrot Playing the Guitar 13
Pollock, Jackson 35
Pop art 41, 44
Port Lligat 20, 22, 36
Portrait of Luis Buñuel 11
Portrait of My Father 9
Poussin, Nicolas 30
Prado, the (museum) 10

Rivera, Miguel Primo de 12, 20
Roman Catholicism 6, 17, 24, 36,
    44

Sagrada Familia (church) 8
San Fernando Academy of Fine
    Arts 10, 12, 14
Schiaparelli, Elsa 28
The Secret Life of Salvador Dalí 7,
    32, 34
Spanish Civil War, 24-25, 26, 28,
    32, 43
stereoscopy 38
Surrealism and the Surrealists 10,
    16, 18-19, 28, 30, 32, 42-43, 44
Surrealist manifestoes 12, 18, 20, 42

Theatre-Museum 38, 45
'Theory of Relativity' 20, 21

unconscious mind 18, 27, 30, 36, 42, 44
United States 22, 32, 34-35, 36

Velázquez, Diego 10
Vermeer, Jan 14, 15

Warhol, Andy 41
*Woman at a Window Sewing in
    Figueres* 14, 15
World War II 32, 35